Part 1: The Descent

Chapter 1: The Crime

Setting the Scene

Mark Daniels was a man of simple means, working as a mechanic in a small California town. He was known for his skill with engines, his easy smile, and his dedication to his family. Mark loved his wife, Sarah, and their two young daughters, Emma and Lily, more than anything. But life had not been kind to the Daniels family. Mounting medical bills from Lily's complicated birth, coupled with the slow business at the garage where Mark worked, had put them under severe financial strain.

Every day, Mark would come home to the small, two-bedroom house they rented on the edge of town, weary from work but trying to muster a smile for his family. The girls were too young to understand the gravity of their situation, but Sarah saw the weight on Mark's shoulders. They would often sit in the kitchen after the children were asleep, discussing their dwindling savings and the growing pile of bills.

One evening, after another disappointing day at work, Mark received a call from an old acquaintance, Trevor, who he hadn't seen in years. Trevor had been in and out of trouble since high school, always looking for the next quick buck. He now claimed to have a surefire way for Mark to make some easy money. Mark was skeptical but also desperate. He agreed to meet Trevor, hoping for a legitimate opportunity, though deep down, he feared the worst.

The Decision

At their meeting, Trevor outlined a plan to rob a small convenience store on the outskirts of town. He assured Mark it would be a quick and easy job—just scare the clerk, take the money, and leave. Trevor had done his "homework"; the store had minimal security, and the clerk usually worked alone during late hours. The take, while not enormous, would be enough to cover some of Mark's most pressing bills.

Mark sat in stunned silence, grappling with the enormity of what was being proposed. The idea of committing a crime went against everything he believed in, everything he had ever stood for. Yet, the image of his family struggling, of his daughters going without, weighed heavily on him. Trevor, sensing Mark's hesitation, played on his fears, painting a picture of the future if Mark continued to do nothing—more bills, more debt, and the possibility of losing their home.

Faced with what seemed like an impossible choice, Mark felt trapped. His pride and desperation clashed violently within him. On one hand, he despised the idea of stooping to criminal activity; on the other, he felt a fierce need to protect his family from hardship. Trevor's words echoed in his mind, mingling with his own fears and anxieties. The rational part of him knew it was wrong, yet the weight of his circumstances pushed him towards the edge.

Ultimately, in a moment of weakness and despair, Mark agreed to participate in the robbery. He rationalized it as a one-time mistake, something that would allow him to get back on his feet and take care of his family. He convinced himself that he could handle the guilt, that the ends would justify the means.

The Robbery

The night of the robbery arrived sooner than Mark would have liked. As he drove to the rendezvous point, his mind was a storm of thoughts and emotions. He thought of Sarah and the girls, imagining their faces if they knew what he was about to do. His stomach churned with a mix of fear and guilt, but he pushed these feelings down, focusing instead on the plan.

Trevor was waiting outside the store, wearing a hooded sweatshirt and dark jeans. He handed Mark a mask and a gun, the weight of the weapon feeling alien and heavy in Mark's hand. His heart raced as he followed Trevor into the store, the bell above the door chiming a light, cheery tone that seemed absurdly out of place.

The clerk, a young man in his early twenties, looked up from the counter, eyes widening in surprise. Trevor barked orders, demanding money while brandishing his weapon. Mark, his voice shaky, echoed Trevor's demands, his eyes darting around the store, looking for exits, witnesses, anything that could go wrong.

The plan began to unravel when the clerk, hands trembling, fumbled with the cash register. Trevor, losing patience, stepped forward aggressively. In the chaos, Mark's grip tightened on the gun, his finger slipping onto the trigger. The gun went off, the sound deafening in the confined space. The clerk screamed, dropping to the floor, and Mark stood frozen, the reality of what he had done crashing down on him.

The gunshot hadn't hit anyone, but it shattered the fragile control Mark had over the situation. In the panicked moments that followed, they grabbed whatever cash they could and fled the scene, leaving the terrified clerk behind. As they drove away, Mark could barely hear Trevor's frantic shouting over the roaring in his ears.

The rush of adrenaline left Mark shaken and nauseous. He had crossed a line, one he had never imagined crossing. The realization of what he had done, the fear he had inflicted, and the sheer recklessness of the act settled over him like a suffocating blanket. As they parted ways, Trevor seemed exhilarated, but Mark felt only a hollow, gnawing regret.

Returning home that night, Mark washed the smell of gunpowder and sweat from his hands, the water scalding but failing to cleanse his conscience. He lay awake, staring at the ceiling, haunted by the memory of the clerk's face and the sound of the gunshot. He knew that no amount of money could justify what he had done, and the fear of what might come next—arrest, imprisonment, losing his family—loomed large in his mind.

As he drifted into a restless sleep, Mark couldn't shake the feeling that he had irrevocably changed the course of his life, that he was now caught in a web of consequences far beyond his control. The weight of his actions pressed down on him, the gravity of his choice pulling him into a deep, dark abyss.

Chapter 2: The Arrest and Trial

The Arrest

It was a dreary morning when Mark's world came crashing down. The sound of heavy footsteps and the pounding on the door jolted him awake. He had barely managed to close his eyes for a few hours, his mind still reeling from the events of the previous night. Groggy and disoriented, he stumbled out of bed, hoping against hope that this was some kind of nightmare.

Sarah, who had been restless as well, followed Mark to the front door. She opened it to find a line of police officers standing there, their expressions grim and determined. Mark's heart sank as he realized the gravity of the situation. The officers pushed past him into the house, their presence filling the small living room with an intimidating authority.

"Mark Daniels?" one of the officers asked.

Mark nodded, his throat dry. "Yes, that's me."

Without another word, the officers moved to cuff him, the cold metal of the handcuffs biting into his wrists. He looked around, seeing Sarah's stunned face, her eyes wide with a mix of fear and confusion. Emma and Lily, barely understanding the commotion, stood clutching their mother's legs, their innocent eyes darting between the officers and their father.

"What's happening?" Sarah's voice trembled, her gaze locked on Mark.

"They're arresting him," an officer explained tersely. "For his involvement in a robbery."

Sarah's face went pale, and she sank into the couch, her hands covering her mouth as tears welled up in her eyes. Emma and Lily began to cry, sensing their mother's distress but not understanding why their father was being taken away. The noise and confusion were overwhelming for them, a sharp contrast to the quiet life they had known.

Mark tried to reach out to Sarah, his heart breaking at the sight of her pain. "Sarah, I—I'm so sorry. I didn't—"

His words were cut off as the officers guided him out the door, leaving his family behind in a whirlwind of sorrow and confusion. As Mark was led to the patrol car, he glanced back one last time, his heart heavy with guilt. The sight of Sarah holding their daughters, her shoulders shaking with sobs, was etched into his mind as the car doors shut behind him.

Legal Proceedings

The trial unfolded with a speed that left Mark reeling. In the weeks following his arrest, Mark found himself facing a court that seemed more interested in swift justice than in understanding his situation. The evidence against him was overwhelming: surveillance footage from the convenience store, the witness statements, and his own confession when he was arrested.

Mark's court-appointed lawyer, Mr. Jensen, tried his best to mount a defense. He argued for leniency, highlighting Mark's lack of a prior criminal record and his difficult circumstances. Mr. Jensen painted a picture of a man driven to desperate measures, emphasizing Mark's genuine remorse and the extreme financial pressure that had led him to make such a grave error.

Despite these efforts, the prosecution's case was strong. The footage of the robbery, combined with the emotional testimony of the store clerk, painted a clear and distressing picture of Mark's involvement. The clerk's statements about the terror he had experienced, and the subsequent news reports detailing the event, painted Mark in an increasingly negative light.

The trial was a blur of legal jargon and heated arguments. Mark's hope of a reduced sentence dwindled with each passing day. As the verdict was read—guilty on all counts—the reality of his situation sank in with a crushing weight. The judge's gavel struck with a finality that echoed in Mark's mind, sentencing him to ten years in prison.

Family Reactions

The news of Mark's sentence hit his family hard. Sarah was left to grapple with the overwhelming burden of managing their household alone, while trying to explain the situation to Emma and Lily in a way they could understand. The financial strain that had driven Mark to commit the crime was now compounded by the legal fees and the cost of maintaining the household on a single income.

Sarah struggled to maintain a semblance of normalcy for their daughters. She put on a brave face for their sake, but the cracks were visible. Friends and extended family offered sympathy, but there was little they could do to ease the burden Sarah faced. The emotional toll was evident in her weary eyes and the lines etched deeper into her face.

The estrangement began to take its toll on Sarah and Mark's relationship. Initially, Sarah visited Mark regularly, trying to support him and maintain a connection for the sake of their children. But as the visits became more infrequent and the letters less frequent, the emotional distance grew. Sarah's frustration and anger were directed not just at Mark for his actions, but also at the circumstances that had left her alone to deal with everything.

Emma and Lily, who had once clung to their father with unreserved love, began to struggle with their emotions. Emma, being older, asked difficult questions about why her father was in prison and why their family had changed so drastically. Lily, too young to fully understand, sensed the shift in their lives and reacted with confusion and occasional outbursts of anger.

Mark's letters from prison were filled with heartfelt apologies and attempts to explain his actions, but they were often met with silence. Sarah's letters were increasingly short and distant, reflecting the strain that the separation had placed on their relationship. The once close-knit family was now fractured, each member dealing with the fallout of Mark's crime in their own way.

As Mark settled into his new reality, he began to confront the profound impact of his actions. The guilt of causing his family such pain and the regret of missing out on precious years with his daughters loomed large over him. The road ahead seemed bleak, with ten years stretching out before him and no clear path back to the life he once knew.

In the depths of his confinement, Mark was left to reflect on the choices that had led him to this point, grappling with the consequences of his actions and the shattered dreams of a once-promising future.

Chapter 3: Arrival in Prison

Intake Process

The prison gates loomed large, their rusting bars a stark reminder of the reality Mark Daniels was about to face. As the prison transport bus rolled through the security checkpoint, Mark's thoughts were a tumultuous mix of fear, anxiety, and resignation. The bus came to a halt, and he was led into a cavernous, sterile intake area, where the first steps of his new life were about to begin.

The intake process was dehumanizing. Mark was stripped of his personal identity and reduced to a mere number. He was instructed to remove his clothes and submit to a thorough search. Every aspect of his individuality was erased, from his worn-out jeans to the family photo he had kept in his wallet. His clothes were replaced with a standard-issue prison uniform, and a number was stamped on a small metal tag that was pinned to his shirt.

Mark felt a profound sense of loss as he watched his belongings being bagged up and labeled for storage. The moment the tag was fastened to his uniform, he was no longer Mark Daniels; he was Inmate #45321. The reality of his situation began to sink in, the weight of the number on his chest a stark reminder of his new, impersonal existence.

Initial Fear and Isolation

The next few hours were a blur of processing and orientation. Mark was taken to a large, echoing room where he was assigned a bunk and given a brief overview of the prison rules and regulations. The prison's cold, clinical environment was a stark contrast to the warmth of his home. The constant hum of fluorescent lights and the distant clanging of metal only added to his sense of disorientation.

As he walked through the crowded corridors to his cell, Mark's anxiety was palpable. He looked at the faces of the other inmates, trying to gauge their intentions. Some seemed indifferent, while others observed him with a calculating gaze. The atmosphere was thick with unspoken tension and unending noise—a cacophony of voices, clanging doors, and shuffling feet.

The small, cramped cell he was assigned to felt like a cage. It contained little more than a metal bunk bed, a tiny sink, and a toilet with no privacy. Mark's first night in the cell was sleepless. He lay on the hard mattress, staring up at the narrow window high above him, feeling the oppressive weight of his confinement. The thin blanket did little to ward off the cold, and the constant shuffling of footsteps and muffled conversations from the adjacent cells kept him awake.

Fear gnawed at Mark as he contemplated his future. His mind raced with thoughts of how he would survive in this hostile environment. He worried about his safety, knowing that prison was a place where the strong preyed on the weak. The harsh reality of his isolation was stark—no friends, no family, just a sea of strangers in a world that seemed alien and unforgiving.

The initial days were a test of endurance. Mark struggled with the sheer isolation from his family and the outside world. His letters home had been few and far between, and each day without a response felt like a dagger to his heart. The distance and lack of communication only deepened his sense of loneliness.

The Harsh Realities of Prison Life

Mark's days quickly fell into a monotonous routine. The prison schedule was rigid, with early wake-up calls, mandatory roll calls, and strict meal times. The limited time allowed for exercise or recreation was often overshadowed by the constant surveillance and lack of privacy. The little freedom he once took for granted was now a distant memory.

The interactions with fellow inmates were fraught with tension. Mark had to navigate a delicate balance between appearing strong enough to avoid being targeted and not drawing undue attention. The unwritten rules of the prison world were complex and ever-shifting, with power dynamics that seemed almost impossible to decipher. He learned quickly that staying under the radar was often the best way to avoid trouble.

The prison guards, while not overtly hostile, were indifferent to the plight of the inmates. They followed protocols with a mechanical efficiency, often treating inmates as mere numbers rather than human beings. Mark's interactions with them were brief and functional, centered around compliance with rules and regulations.

Despite his best efforts to keep his head down, Mark was constantly reminded of his circumstances. The echo of cell doors slamming shut, the shouting of orders, and the distant cries of frustration and anger from other inmates were a constant reminder of the harsh environment he now inhabited. He began to feel the weight of his actions more acutely, the isolation and confinement amplifying his remorse.

Coping Mechanisms

Mark sought solace in small routines and coping mechanisms. He focused on maintaining personal hygiene and organizing his cell as best as he could. He found a small measure of comfort in reading the prison library's meager selection of books and writing letters to Sarah and his daughters, despite the growing distance between them.

Art became a refuge for Mark. He began sketching in his free time, using whatever materials he could scrounge up. The process of creating something, even in such a bleak environment, provided a temporary escape from his harsh reality. It was a way for him to channel his emotions and regain a sense of control amidst the chaos.

As the days turned into weeks, Mark slowly began to adapt to his new reality. He learned to navigate the prison's complex social structure and found ways to protect himself. The fear and anxiety that had initially overwhelmed him began to temper with a hard-earned resilience. He started to understand that survival in prison was not just about physical endurance but also about mental fortitude.

Through it all, Mark held on to the hope that he could make something positive out of his time in prison. The memories of his family and the desire to better himself became his guiding light, pushing him to endure the harsh realities of prison life with a measure of hope and determination.

Part 2: Survival

Chapter 4: Life in Prison

Adapting to the Environment

Mark Daniels quickly learned that survival in prison required more than just enduring the harsh conditions; it demanded an understanding of the complex social hierarchy that dictated life behind bars. The prison's environment was a microcosm of power dynamics and social structures, each layer as impenetrable and unforgiving as the walls that enclosed him.

On his first day, Mark observed the unspoken rules of the prison. He saw how inmates fell into various groups and cliques, each with its own set of behaviors and codes of conduct. There were the long-term residents who had become almost institutionalized, the newly arrived who were still finding their footing, and the transient inmates who passed through like shadows.

Mark quickly realized that understanding who to avoid was crucial. Certain inmates were known for their aggressive behavior and predatory tendencies. He learned to identify them by their interactions and the fear they instilled in others. The prison had its own form of pecking order, where the most feared and influential individuals often wielded a type of informal power. Mark stayed clear of these individuals, focusing instead on blending in and avoiding conflict.

At the same time, Mark tried to build a small network of acquaintances. He engaged with inmates who seemed less volatile and more focused on their own survival and rehabilitation. These connections, while tenuous, provided him with valuable information and a semblance of support. It became clear that while friendship was rare and often fleeting, alliances and mutual respect could provide some degree of security.

Mark also took steps to protect himself physically. He learned to read the body language and subtle cues that signaled impending trouble. He became proficient at defusing potential conflicts through calm and measured responses, often retreating from confrontations rather than escalating them. His instincts and adaptability were put to the test daily, and he found that maintaining a low profile was often his best defense.

Daily Routine

The daily routine in prison was a relentless cycle of monotony and regimentation. Each day began before dawn, with a blaring alarm signaling the start of a new day. Mark, like all inmates, was required to rise promptly and prepare for the day's activities.

Morning roll call was a mandatory ritual, during which inmates were counted and checked for any contraband. The guards conducted these checks with a mechanical efficiency that left little room for deviation. Mark learned to comply with their demands quickly and without complaint, knowing that any resistance or mistake could result in punitive measures.

Meals were served in a large, communal cafeteria, where the quality of food was often subpar. The atmosphere during meal times was one of constant vigilance. Inmates jostled for space and food, and Mark found himself navigating these interactions with care. He learned to eat quickly and to keep his head down, avoiding eye contact and potential conflicts.

The remainder of the day was structured around a series of scheduled activities. Inmates were assigned to work details, educational programs, or various forms of recreation. Mark was assigned to a maintenance crew, where he performed menial tasks around the prison. The work was physically demanding but provided a small measure of autonomy and the chance to stay active.

Mark's interactions with the guards were a mix of wary respect and cautious compliance. The guards were generally indifferent to the inmates' personal struggles but were quick to enforce rules and regulations. Mark learned to navigate these interactions with a blend of deference and assertiveness, understanding that maintaining a respectful demeanor was often the best way to avoid trouble.

Despite the rigid structure, Mark found moments of respite in small personal routines. He used his limited free time to write letters, read, and engage in solitary activities that provided a brief escape from the prison's harsh realities. These moments were crucial for his mental well-being, allowing him to maintain a sense of normalcy amid the unrelenting demands of prison life.

Adapting to the System

Mark's adaptation to the prison system was a continuous process of trial and error. He learned to navigate the bureaucracy of the prison's administrative system, understanding how to request necessary items, file grievances, and access available resources. His experience with the prison's rigid routines and regulations was a lesson in patience and perseverance.

He also began to understand the informal economy that existed within the prison. Inmates traded goods and services in a system that operated outside of official channels. Mark saw opportunities to trade his artistic creations for items he needed or for small favors, finding that his ability to draw and create art could provide him with a modest but valuable source of income.

The psychological impact of prison life was profound. Mark grappled with feelings of isolation and the constant strain of his circumstances. He found solace in his art, which became both a means of financial survival and a therapeutic outlet for his emotions. The process of creating art allowed him to channel his feelings of regret and hope into something tangible, providing a brief respite from the harsh environment.

Mark's journey in prison was one of continuous adjustment and survival. The harsh realities of prison life were tempered by his determination to find a way through the adversity. Each day was a test of endurance and resilience, but Mark's ability to adapt and navigate the complex dynamics of prison life allowed him to find a sense of stability in the midst of chaos.

Chapter 5: The Art of Survival

Discovering Art

Mark Daniels' first few months in prison were marked by a numbing routine of work, meals, and limited recreation. Amidst the drudgery, he struggled to find a sense of purpose and escape from the relentless monotony of prison life. One afternoon, while cleaning a storage room as part of his work detail, Mark came across a stack of discarded art supplies—old sketchbooks, colored pencils, and paints.

The sight of these materials stirred a long-buried memory. As a child and teenager, Mark had harbored a passion for drawing and painting, a creative outlet he had set aside as life's responsibilities took over. The memory of those simpler times, when art had been his escape from the challenges of adolescence, resurfaced with a surprising intensity. The discovery of the art supplies in the prison's storage room felt like a sign—a chance to reconnect with a part of himself he had nearly forgotten.

With a mixture of nostalgia and curiosity, Mark took the supplies back to his cell. He started tentatively, sketching simple shapes and practicing techniques he had long neglected. The process of drawing became a meditative escape from his grim surroundings. Each line and stroke on the paper was a small victory against the oppressive environment that surrounded him.

Mark's rediscovery of art was more than a pastime; it was a lifeline. He began to explore different mediums and techniques, immersing himself in the act of creation. The cell, once a symbol of confinement, transformed into a studio where he could express himself freely. The art became a way to channel his emotions, his regrets, and his hope for redemption into something beautiful.

Selling Art

As Mark's skill and confidence grew, so did his realization of the potential value of his artwork. The prison economy, a microcosm of commerce and trade, operated on a barter system where goods and services were exchanged for items like commissary credits, hygiene products, and even favors. Mark saw an opportunity to leverage his artistic talent to improve his quality of life and gain some measure of control over his circumstances.

He began to trade his artwork for commissary items. Initially, it was a small-scale operation. He would sketch simple portraits or landscapes and offer them in exchange for basic necessities—extra soap, better-quality food, or even stamps for his letters. The value of his art as a currency became apparent as inmates began to seek him out for custom pieces.

Word of Mark's artwork spread throughout the prison, and he soon found himself inundated with requests. Inmates asked for personalized drawings of family members, portraits of loved ones, or elaborate designs for tattoos. Each commission was an opportunity to not only earn valuable items but also to connect with others on a personal level. Through his art, Mark was able to create a bridge between himself and the other inmates, establishing a niche for himself in the prison's informal economy.

The trade also introduced Mark to a new set of social dynamics. He learned to navigate the complexities of the prison barter system, understanding the value of his work and how to negotiate fair exchanges. His artwork became a commodity in high demand, and he developed relationships with various inmates who became regular clients. These relationships, while often transactional, provided Mark with a sense of community and a small measure of respect within the prison.

The Transformative Power of Art

The process of creating and trading art had a profound effect on Mark's mental and emotional well-being. It provided him with a sense of purpose and accomplishment, offering a reprieve from the relentless monotony of prison life. The act of creating something beautiful allowed him to reconnect with his own humanity and find solace in his talent.

Mark's artistic pursuits also offered him a unique form of rehabilitation. Through art, he was able to confront and express his feelings of guilt, regret, and hope for redemption. The work he produced was a testament to his journey, a visual representation of his internal struggles and aspirations. The act of drawing and painting became a form of therapy, helping him to process his emotions and find a sense of peace amidst the chaos.

In addition to the personal benefits, Mark's art began to make an impact on the prison community. His creations were displayed in common areas, providing a rare glimpse of beauty in the harsh environment. The positive responses from other inmates and even some guards were a testament to the transformative power of art. It became a source of inspiration and a symbol of hope, demonstrating that even in the most challenging circumstances, creativity and resilience could thrive.

Mark's journey through prison was far from easy, but his rediscovery of art played a crucial role in his survival and personal growth. The process of creating and trading artwork not only provided him with practical benefits but also helped him to navigate the complexities of prison life with a renewed sense of purpose. Through his art, Mark found a way to transcend the limitations of his environment and forge a path toward redemption and self-discovery.

Chapter 6: The Isolation

Loss of Contact

The first few months in prison had been a whirlwind of adjustment and survival. As Mark settled into his new routine and found solace in his art, he faced a new and profound challenge: the growing distance from his family. The letters he had sent home, filled with apologies, updates, and expressions of love, began to go unanswered. Days turned into weeks, and weeks into months, with no word from Sarah or their daughters.

The infrequent visits that had once been a lifeline grew increasingly rare. Sarah, overwhelmed by the weight of managing their family and coping with the financial strain, struggled to keep up with the demands of prison visits. The logistical challenges of making the long trip to the prison, combined with the emotional toll of seeing Mark behind bars, made each visit more difficult for her.

Mark's attempts to bridge the gap through letters seemed futile. Each envelope he received, with its official prison stamp, was met with disappointment when it contained only updates on his case or official notices. The silence from his family was a constant ache, a gnawing reminder of the distance that had grown between them.

The isolation Mark felt was not just physical but deeply emotional. The lack of communication with his loved ones left him feeling abandoned and disconnected. He often found himself staring at the blank pages of his cell, trying to find the right words to express his thoughts and feelings, only to be met with the realization that his efforts seemed to go unnoticed. The void left by his family's silence was a painful reminder of the consequences of his actions.

Internal Struggles

The emotional weight of isolation bore heavily on Mark's psyche. The silence from his family and the rare, distant visits intensified his feelings of guilt and remorse. Mark's mind frequently returned to thoughts of his family, particularly his daughters, who were growing up without their father. The pain of separation was compounded by the constant reminder of his role in their suffering.

His daughter's memory, especially, was a source of deep anguish. He often revisited the fleeting memories of her infancy, the brief moments he had with her before she passed away. The loss of her presence was a heavy burden, one that he grappled with daily. Mark was haunted by the thought of what might have been—her laughter, her milestones, the chance to be a part of her life. The guilt of not being there for her, and for the family he had left behind, was a constant weight on his conscience.

Mark's thoughts were a swirl of regret and self-recrimination. He wrestled with questions about how he could have made different choices, how he might have avoided the path that led him to prison. His introspection was a tumultuous journey through his own mistakes and the pain he had inflicted on those he loved. The sense of isolation from his family amplified these struggles, making it difficult for him to find peace or solace.

The emotional void left by his family's absence was filled with the harsh realities of prison life. The constant noise and the unrelenting nature of his environment offered little respite from his internal turmoil. Mark's art became both a refuge and a reminder of his circumstances. While creating art provided a temporary escape, it also served as a mirror to his feelings of loss and regret. Each piece he completed was a reflection of his inner struggles and his longing for redemption.

Guilt and Reflection

Mark's reflections on his past were often tinged with a profound sense of guilt. He thought about the decisions that had led him to this point, the choices made under pressure and the devastating consequences that followed. The thought of his family's suffering, and the impact of his actions on their lives, was a constant source of anguish.

He grappled with the realization that his mistakes had not only cost him his freedom but had also fractured the lives of those he loved. The isolation from his family was a painful reminder of the distance he had created between himself and his loved ones. Mark was left to confront the full scope of his actions and their repercussions, a process that was both painful and necessary for his own growth and redemption.

In his quiet moments, Mark often found himself questioning the nature of forgiveness and whether he would ever be able to earn it, both from his family and from himself. The journey of self-forgiveness was a difficult one, fraught with the realization of his past mistakes and the challenge of reconciling them with the man he hoped to become.

The isolation Mark experienced was not just a physical separation but a profound emotional and psychological struggle. The silence from his family, the weight of his guilt, and the harsh realities of prison life combined to create a complex and often painful internal landscape. Yet, amidst the struggle, Mark's commitment to finding redemption and making amends for his past actions remained a guiding force, driving him to continue his journey of self-improvement and personal growth.

Chapter 7: Mentorship Begins

Becoming a Mentor

As Mark Daniels settled into the rhythms of prison life, he began to recognize an opportunity to contribute to the community around him in a meaningful way. Having found some semblance of stability through his art and daily routines, he sought a new purpose beyond mere survival. The idea of mentoring new inmates appealed to him not only as a way to give back but also as a path to redemption and self-improvement.

Mark's initial steps into mentorship were modest. He started by informally helping newcomers who seemed lost or overwhelmed. His approach was grounded in his own experiences; he shared practical advice on navigating the prison system, finding resources, and understanding the informal social dynamics. These initial interactions were often brief but valuable, as he provided guidance on everything from dealing with the guards to managing personal safety.

Recognizing the positive impact he could have, Mark began to formalize his role. He sought out opportunities to connect with new arrivals and offer more structured support. Mark reached out to prison counselors and expressed his interest in mentoring, highlighting his own experiences and the lessons he had learned. To his surprise, his proposal was met with cautious approval. The prison administration was open to the idea of inmates helping each other, as long as it was monitored closely.

Mark was officially recognized as a mentor, a role that came with responsibilities and a certain degree of respect. He was assigned to work with new inmates who were struggling to adapt to prison life. The mentorship program was designed to provide guidance and support, helping new arrivals find their footing and avoid common pitfalls.

Challenges

Mentorship, however, was far from straightforward. Mark faced numerous challenges as he began his new role. One of the primary obstacles was overcoming the resistance and mistrust from other inmates. Many new arrivals were wary of advice from a fellow prisoner, especially one who was still grappling with his own struggles and regrets.

The initial reactions to Mark's attempts at mentorship were mixed. Some inmates viewed him with suspicion, questioning his motives and the authenticity of his intentions. They were accustomed to a culture of self-preservation and distrust, where trust was hard-earned and often fleeting. Mark had to work diligently to build rapport and demonstrate that his guidance was genuine and intended to help, not to exploit or manipulate.

In addition to resistance from the new inmates, Mark also encountered challenges from the established prison hierarchy. Some long-term residents viewed his role with skepticism, seeing it as an attempt to gain favor or exert influence. These inmates were often quick to challenge Mark's authority and question his motives. Mark had to navigate these power dynamics carefully, ensuring that his actions were seen as supportive rather than as attempts to undermine the existing social order.

Dealing with the emotional and psychological needs of the new inmates was another significant challenge. Many were struggling with their own issues, including feelings of fear, anger, and despair. Mark found himself providing not only practical advice but also emotional support. The process was emotionally draining, as he had to balance his own struggles with the needs of others. He frequently encountered inmates who were resistant to change or unwilling to accept help, which tested his patience and resilience.

Despite these challenges, Mark remained committed to his role as a mentor. He understood that building trust and credibility would take time. He focused on being consistent, reliable, and empathetic, demonstrating through his actions that he genuinely cared about the well-being of those he was helping.

Mark also faced difficulties in managing his own emotions while guiding others. The process of mentoring often forced him to confront his own regrets and insecurities. He had to navigate the fine line between being supportive and maintaining his own boundaries, ensuring that he did not become overwhelmed by the emotional weight of others' problems.

Growth and Impact

Through perseverance and dedication, Mark gradually began to see positive results from his mentorship efforts. Inmates who had initially been skeptical of him started to appreciate his guidance and support. Mark's approach, which combined practical advice with empathy and understanding, began to resonate with those he was helping.

The transformation was gradual but noticeable. Some of the new inmates began to adapt to prison life more effectively, finding ways to cope with the challenges they faced. Mark's mentorship not only provided them with practical tools for survival but also offered them a sense of hope and connection in an otherwise isolating environment.

Mark's own growth was also evident. The experience of mentoring others helped him to develop a greater sense of purpose and self-worth. It allowed him to channel his own experiences and struggles into a positive force for change. The process of helping others navigate their own challenges provided him with a renewed sense of meaning and contributed to his personal healing.

In the end, Mark's role as a mentor became a vital part of his journey toward redemption. It was a testament to his commitment to improving himself and contributing positively to his community. Despite the challenges and setbacks, Mark found that his efforts had a meaningful impact, both on the lives of the inmates he mentored and on his own path to personal growth.

Part 3: Transformation

Chapter 8: Education and Growth

Enrolling in Education

Mark Daniels had settled into his role as a mentor and found a measure of stability through his art, but he knew that his journey toward transformation required more than just external adjustments. He realized that to truly change himself and his circumstances, he needed to focus on personal growth and intellectual development. The prison's education program offered a structured path to achieve this, and Mark saw it as an opportunity to reshape his future.

The education program in prison was a lifeline for many inmates, providing a range of courses from basic literacy to advanced studies. Mark began by enrolling in foundational classes, starting with subjects like mathematics and basic English. These initial courses were designed to address the educational gaps that many inmates had, including Mark. The material was often basic, but for Mark, it was a crucial step toward more complex learning.

As he progressed, Mark showed a keen interest in expanding his education. He took advantage of every opportunity to enroll in more advanced courses. His dedication and enthusiasm did not go unnoticed; instructors and prison staff saw his commitment and supported his efforts. Mark's academic journey became a source of motivation for him, a way to reclaim control over his life and build a foundation for the future.

The structure of the education program required him to manage his time effectively, balancing his studies with his responsibilities as a mentor and his work details. Mark embraced this challenge, finding that the discipline required for academic success complemented the discipline he had cultivated in other areas of his life. His schedule was filled with study sessions, assignments, and exams, all of which contributed to his growing sense of purpose.

Intellectual Awakening

Mark's involvement in the education program sparked an intellectual awakening. As he delved into subjects like history, literature, and social sciences, he found himself increasingly captivated by the world of ideas. The academic material provided him with a new perspective on life, challenging his preconceived notions and broadening his understanding of society and human nature.

His newfound passion for learning was evident in his approach to his studies. Mark became an avid reader, devouring books and articles on a wide range of topics. The prison library, though limited, became a sanctuary where he could explore new ideas and expand his knowledge. He often spent hours absorbed in his studies, losing himself in the pages of books that offered both escape and enlightenment.

The intellectual stimulation provided by his education was transformative. Mark began to see himself not just as an inmate but as a person with potential and aspirations. The process of learning and achieving academic milestones gave him a sense of empowerment that transcended the confines of his environment. His achievements in the education program became a source of immense pride, a tangible sign of his growth and progress.

Mark's academic successes extended beyond his personal satisfaction. His performance in courses earned him recognition and respect within the prison community. Fellow inmates began to see him as a role model for self-improvement, and his journey from a troubled past to academic accomplishment inspired others. Mark's ability to balance his responsibilities and excel in his studies demonstrated that change was possible, even in the most challenging of circumstances.

The knowledge Mark gained through his education had practical implications as well. It equipped him with skills and insights that were valuable both in prison and for his future. His improved literacy and critical thinking skills contributed to his effectiveness as a mentor and allowed him to engage in more meaningful conversations with others. Mark's education became a cornerstone of his transformation, providing him with the tools to navigate his environment with greater confidence and purpose.

Personal Growth and Future Aspirations

The education program was more than just a means of passing time for Mark; it was a crucial component of his personal growth. The intellectual stimulation and academic achievements gave him a renewed sense of direction and hope. He began to envision a future beyond prison, one where his newly acquired knowledge and skills could be applied in positive ways.

Mark's aspirations extended beyond the confines of the prison walls. He started to think about potential career paths and opportunities for continued education after his release. The subjects he studied and the insights he gained inspired him to consider contributing to society in meaningful ways. He dreamed of using his education to advocate for criminal justice reform, support others who had faced similar struggles, and continue his artistic pursuits.

The transformation Mark underwent through his education was a testament to his resilience and determination. He had turned a challenging environment into a platform for growth and self-discovery. His journey from a man grappling with guilt and isolation to an empowered and knowledgeable individual was a powerful narrative of redemption.

Mark's education and intellectual awakening were integral to his overall transformation. They provided him with a sense of purpose, a renewed self-worth, and a vision for the future. As he continued to navigate the complexities of prison life, his academic achievements remained a source of pride and a beacon of hope, guiding him toward a brighter and more fulfilling future.

Chapter 9: Self-Help and Therapy

Joining Self-Help Groups

As part of his ongoing transformation, Mark Daniels took the significant step of joining self-help groups offered within the prison. These groups were designed to address various aspects of personal development and rehabilitation, and Mark saw them as essential components of his journey toward redemption.

The prison had several self-help and therapeutic programs, each targeting different issues such as anger management, substance abuse, and personal growth. Mark initially attended an anger management group, which focused on helping inmates understand and control their emotions. The group provided a structured environment where participants could share their experiences, learn coping strategies, and work on rebuilding their emotional regulation.

Mark was hesitant at first, unsure of what to expect from the sessions. The group was composed of individuals from various backgrounds, each with their own struggles and stories. As he began to participate, he found that the group's discussions were both challenging and enlightening. The process of confronting his own emotions and listening to others' experiences provided a broader perspective on the nature of anger and its impact.

In addition to anger management, Mark joined a rehabilitation support group that focused on personal growth and accountability. This group aimed to help inmates understand the underlying causes of their criminal behavior and develop strategies for positive change. The sessions involved deep self-reflection, discussion of past actions, and exploration of personal values and goals.

Mark's involvement in these groups became a crucial part of his rehabilitation. They provided him with a safe space to explore his emotions and confront the underlying issues that had contributed to his criminal behavior. The structured nature of the groups, combined with the support of fellow inmates, helped him to develop a more nuanced understanding of himself and his actions.

Facing Demons

The self-help groups offered Mark an opportunity to face his inner demons and confront the guilt and shame associated with his past actions. The process of sharing his story with others, and listening to their experiences, brought to light many of the underlying factors that had influenced his decisions and behavior.

Mark's participation in the groups was often emotionally taxing. The process of revisiting the details of his crime, the impact on his family, and the choices that led him to prison was a painful experience. He grappled with intense feelings of guilt and shame, struggling to reconcile his past actions with the person he was becoming.

During one particularly intense session, Mark shared the story of the robbery gone wrong and the subsequent impact on his life. He spoke about his regrets, the pain of being separated from his family, and the emotional toll of his actions. The vulnerability of this disclosure was both cathartic and uncomfortable. It forced him to confront the reality of his behavior and the consequences it had on those around him.

The support of the group members played a crucial role in Mark's journey. The collective experience of the group, combined with the guidance of the facilitators, helped him to process his emotions and develop a deeper understanding of his motivations. Mark began to recognize patterns in his behavior and the ways in which his past decisions had been influenced by underlying fears and insecurities.

The sessions provided a sense of catharsis, allowing Mark to release some of the emotional weight he had been carrying. As he worked through his feelings of guilt and shame, he also began to develop a sense of self-forgiveness. This process was not immediate, and there were moments of doubt and struggle, but it marked a significant step in his personal growth.

Mark's journey through self-help and therapy also included setting goals for his future. The groups encouraged participants to think about their aspirations and the steps they needed to take to achieve them. Mark began to outline a vision for his life beyond prison, focusing on how he could use his experiences and newfound knowledge to make a positive impact.

The work he did in the self-help groups was a critical part of his transformation. It provided him with the tools and insights needed to confront his past and build a foundation for a more constructive future. The process of facing his demons, coupled with the support and guidance from others, helped Mark to develop a greater sense of self-awareness and a more profound commitment to personal change.

As Mark continued his involvement in the self-help groups, he found that the experience was instrumental in shaping his path to redemption. It offered him a framework for understanding his past, addressing his emotional struggles, and moving forward with a renewed sense of purpose and responsibility.

Chapter 10: The Power of Art

Art as Expression

As Mark Daniels continued to navigate his journey through prison, art became more than just a hobby—it became a vital form of expression and a powerful tool for personal transformation. The emotional depth and complexity of his experiences began to manifest in his artwork, turning his inner turmoil into a visual narrative of redemption, loss, and hope.

Mark's art evolved significantly over time. Initially, his work had been a means of escape, a way to occupy his time and find a modicum of peace in the midst of his challenging environment. But as he delved deeper into his own emotional landscape and experiences, his art began to reflect a more profound and introspective journey.

His pieces started to embody the themes he was grappling with. Redemption was a recurring motif, depicted through imagery of new beginnings and second chances. His paintings often featured symbolic representations of growth and renewal, such as emerging from darkness into light or overcoming obstacles. The process of creating these pieces was both therapeutic and revelatory, allowing Mark to confront his feelings and aspirations in a tangible way.

Loss was another central theme in Mark's art. His work poignantly captured the pain of separation from his family and the sorrow of his daughter's passing. Through hauntingly beautiful portraits and somber landscapes, he expressed the depth of his grief and the void left by his absence in his loved ones' lives. These pieces were raw and emotional, resonating deeply with anyone who viewed them.

Hope, however, was the most transformative theme in Mark's art. His later works depicted scenes of possibility and optimism, reflecting his newfound belief in the possibility of redemption and change. Bright colors, uplifting imagery, and representations of personal triumph became central elements of his creations. Art became a medium through which Mark could envision a future beyond the prison walls, a future filled with potential and renewal.

Mark's art not only served as a personal outlet but also became a way for him to communicate his journey to others. Each piece was a reflection of his internal struggles and growth, offering a glimpse into the complexity of his transformation. His work provided a visual representation of the lessons he had learned and the changes he had undergone.

External Recognition

The quality and emotional depth of Mark's artwork did not go unnoticed. His pieces began to attract attention within the prison community and eventually beyond its confines. Initially, his art was displayed in the prison's common areas, where it drew admiration from fellow inmates and staff. The positive feedback and encouragement he received bolstered his confidence and motivated him to continue his creative pursuits.

The breakthrough came when a prison volunteer, an art enthusiast and local gallery owner, took notice of Mark's work. Impressed by the depth and quality of the pieces, the volunteer facilitated an opportunity for Mark to showcase his art in a local exhibition. This was a pivotal moment for Mark, providing a chance for his work to reach a broader audience.

The exhibition was a significant event, not only for Mark but also for the prison community. The gallery displayed several of his paintings, accompanied by descriptions of his journey and the themes explored in his work. The reception was overwhelmingly positive, with visitors and art critics praising the emotional resonance and technical skill of Mark's pieces.

Sales from the exhibition provided Mark with much-needed financial support. The proceeds from his art allowed him to improve his quality of life in prison, giving him access to better commissary items and resources. More importantly, the external recognition of his talent reinforced his sense of self-worth and commitment to change.

The success of the exhibition led to further opportunities for Mark. His art was featured in additional galleries and exhibitions, both locally and in broader circles. Each new exhibition brought with it a fresh wave of recognition and validation. Mark's story and his art became symbols of personal transformation and hope, inspiring others and demonstrating the power of creativity in the face of adversity.

The external recognition also provided Mark with a sense of connection to the outside world. It bridged the gap between his prison experience and the broader community, allowing him to contribute to a larger conversation about redemption and personal growth. His art became a powerful testament to the human spirit's capacity for change and resilience.

Reinforcing Commitment to Change

The impact of Mark's art extended beyond financial support and recognition. It became a cornerstone of his transformation, reinforcing his commitment to personal change and growth. The positive feedback and external validation he received were affirmations of his progress and a reminder of his potential.

Mark's art served as a constant source of inspiration and motivation. The process of creating and sharing his work allowed him to channel his experiences into something constructive and meaningful. It provided him with a sense of purpose and direction, helping him to maintain focus on his goals and aspirations.

The success of his art also inspired Mark to mentor other inmates in creative expression. He began to offer art classes and workshops, sharing his skills and experiences with those who were interested in exploring their own artistic talents. This new role allowed him to give back to the community and further solidified his commitment to positive change.

Through his art, Mark not only transformed his own life but also made a positive impact on those around him. His journey from a man grappling with guilt and isolation to an accomplished artist and mentor was a powerful narrative of redemption. The power of art had provided him with a means of expression, a source of pride, and a connection to a hopeful future.

Chapter 11: A Glimmer of Hope

Letters from Strangers

Mark Daniels had long grown accustomed to the routine of prison life, but a new chapter in his journey began with a series of unexpected letters. These letters came from people he had never met, and their arrival brought a profound shift in his outlook.

The first letter arrived on an otherwise ordinary day. It was from a woman named Emily, whose husband had been a victim of a violent crime years earlier. Emily had seen one of Mark's artworks displayed in a prison art exhibition and had been deeply moved. Her letter expressed gratitude for the emotional depth and honesty in Mark's art, which she felt had offered her a sense of healing and understanding. Emily wrote that seeing the pieces had helped her come to terms with the trauma she had endured and had provided a sense of connection and closure.

The second letter was from a young man named Jake, who had recently been released from prison. Jake had been serving time for a crime related to drug addiction, and he wrote about how Mark's art had inspired him during his own incarceration. He shared his struggles and his journey toward recovery, emphasizing how Mark's artwork had given him hope and a sense of purpose.

Each letter was a poignant reminder of the impact Mark's work was having beyond the prison walls. These messages were filled with personal stories of struggle and triumph, and they each conveyed a deep sense of gratitude for the solace and inspiration Mark's art had provided.

The letters were a lifeline for Mark, offering him a tangible sense of connection to the world outside and reinforcing the value of his efforts. They were a source of comfort and motivation, showing him that his work was making a difference and reaching people in ways he had never imagined.

Hope for Reconciliation

The arrival of these letters sparked a renewed sense of hope in Mark. He began to see the possibility of reconciliation with his family and society in a new light. The emotional support and validation from strangers provided him with a glimmer of hope that his journey of redemption was not in vain and that there might still be a chance to repair the relationships that had been fractured by his actions.

Mark's hope for reconciliation was bolstered by the realization that his art had become a bridge between his past mistakes and a future of positive change. He saw how his work had touched people's lives and helped them find healing, and he began to believe that his own path to redemption was achievable.

With renewed determination, Mark took steps to reach out to his family once more. He drafted another letter to his wife and daughter, sharing the news of the letters he had received and the impact they had had on him. He expressed his ongoing desire to reconnect and be a part of their lives, hoping that his recent efforts and the positive changes he had made would be evident.

Mark also started thinking about how he could use his experiences to contribute positively to society. He began exploring opportunities to engage with community organizations and support groups, aiming to create a network of support and advocacy that could help others who were struggling.

As he reflected on the messages he had received, Mark felt a profound sense of purpose and commitment. The letters from strangers had not only provided him with hope but had also reinforced his belief in the potential for redemption and change. He understood that the journey ahead would be challenging, but the support and encouragement he had received gave him the strength to continue pursuing his goals and seeking reconciliation.

In the quiet moments of his cell, Mark held onto the hope that his efforts to make amends and his desire to rebuild his relationships would be met with understanding and forgiveness. The letters had provided him with a sense of connection and a renewed sense of purpose, fueling his determination to make the most of the opportunities that lay ahead.

The chapter closed with Mark looking out of his cell window, reflecting on the letters and the hope they had inspired. He was filled with a sense of anticipation and determination, ready to face the challenges of his journey with a renewed sense of purpose and a hopeful outlook on the future.

Chapter 12: Family Ties

Reaching Out

As Mark Daniels approached the final years of his sentence, he was driven by a deep desire to reconcile with his estranged family. The letters from strangers had rekindled his hope for rebuilding the relationships that had been shattered by his crime. Determined to bridge the gap between his past mistakes and his present transformation, Mark set out to write heartfelt letters to his wife, Sarah, and his daughter, Lily.

Mark's letter to Sarah was a delicate balance of apology, explanation, and hope. He began by acknowledging the pain and hardship his actions had caused her and their daughter. He expressed profound remorse for the distress and separation they had endured and detailed his journey of self-reflection, education, and artistic growth during his time in prison. Mark wanted Sarah to know that his path to redemption was sincere and that he had worked hard to become a better person. He wrote about the impact of the letters he had received from strangers, illustrating how these messages had given him hope and reinforced his commitment to change. The letter concluded with an earnest plea for understanding and a tentative wish for a future where they might reconnect.

To Lily, who was now a teenager, Mark's letter was both a message of love and an explanation of his actions. He recounted fond memories from her early childhood, sharing how much he missed being a part of her life. Mark talked about his efforts to make amends and his dreams of being a positive influence in her life once more. He explained the significance of his artistic endeavors and how they had helped him find purpose and healing. His hope was that Lily could see the person he was striving to become and that one day they might rebuild their relationship.

Mark put considerable effort into crafting both letters, pouring his emotions into each word. He was acutely aware that these letters might not be received well or might not receive a response at all. The fear of rejection and the uncertainty of how his family would react weighed heavily on him.

Emotional Toll

The process of writing these letters was both cathartic and emotionally draining for Mark. Each word he wrote was a reflection of his deep regret, his longing for reconciliation, and his hope for a second chance. The act of reaching out was a brave step, but it also reopened old wounds and brought to the forefront the pain of his family's absence.

Mark spent long hours in his cell, grappling with the emotional toll of his estrangement. The memories of his family and the pain of their separation were constant companions. The letters had stirred up a whirlwind of emotions, ranging from hope and anticipation to anxiety and sorrow. He often found himself revisiting the moments of happiness he had shared with his wife and daughter, contrasting them with the current reality of his imprisonment.

The uncertainty of his family's response was a source of deep anxiety. Mark feared that his letters might be ignored or met with anger and resentment. The possibility that his family might choose to remain distant was a painful prospect, and he struggled with the emotional burden of this uncertainty. The anticipation of waiting for a response was marked by sleepless nights and restless days, filled with a mix of hope and dread.

Mark also wrestled with feelings of guilt and self-blame. The absence of his family during his time in prison was a constant reminder of the consequences of his actions. He grappled with the reality that he had caused significant pain and disruption in their lives, and the process of seeking reconciliation was fraught with the weight of this realization.

Despite the emotional toll, Mark remained steadfast in his commitment to reaching out. The letters represented a crucial step in his journey toward redemption and a chance to make amends for the hurt he had caused. His hope for a positive response and a potential path to reconciliation provided him with the motivation to persevere, even in the face of his fears and uncertainties.

As he awaited a response from his family, Mark found solace in the small victories of his personal growth and the support he received from the prison community. The process of reaching out to his family was a testament to his commitment to change and his desire to build a future grounded in redemption and connection.

The chapter closed with Mark looking out of his cell window, reflecting on the letters he had sent and the emotional journey they represented. He was filled with a sense of both trepidation and hope, ready to face whatever response might come, and committed to continuing his path toward personal transformation and reconciliation.

Chapter 13: Challenges of Mentorship

Mentorship Difficulties

As Mark Daniels began his role as a mentor within the prison system, he was eager to offer guidance and support to new inmates. He saw mentorship as a way to redeem himself and make a meaningful contribution to the prison community. However, his enthusiasm was quickly met with a series of challenges that tested his resolve.

The first significant hurdle Mark faced was the skepticism and resistance from his mentees. Many of the new inmates were distrustful of him, viewing him as just another convict with his own agenda. Their wariness was rooted in their own experiences and the harsh realities of prison life. Mark's attempts to reach out and provide support were often met with suspicion or outright hostility. Some inmates saw his efforts as disingenuous, questioning whether he was truly committed to helping them or merely trying to elevate his own status within the prison.

One particular instance highlighted the difficulties Mark encountered. A young inmate named Eddie, who had been convicted of drug-related offenses, was especially resistant to Mark's mentorship. Eddie had a history of failed attempts at rehabilitation and was deeply cynical about the prison system. Mark's initial efforts to connect with Eddie were met with hostility, as Eddie viewed Mark's attempts at encouragement as insincere. The interactions were tense, with Eddie often lashing out or dismissing Mark's advice.

In addition to skepticism, Mark faced the challenge of dealing with conflicting personalities and diverse backgrounds among his mentees. Each individual had their own set of struggles, and Mark had to navigate the complexities of their situations while trying to provide effective guidance. The varying degrees of resistance and mistrust among the inmates made it difficult for Mark to establish a meaningful connection with everyone.

Personal Growth

Despite these challenges, Mark's experiences as a mentor became a crucial part of his personal growth. The difficulties he faced forced him to develop new skills and insights that contributed to his ongoing transformation.

1. Learning Patience

One of the most important lessons Mark learned was patience. Working with individuals who were resistant or distrusting required a level of perseverance and calm that Mark had to cultivate. He discovered that building trust and rapport with his mentees was a gradual process that could not be rushed. Mark's patience allowed him to endure the setbacks and continue offering support, even when progress seemed slow.

2. Developing Empathy

Mark's interactions with his mentees also deepened his understanding of empathy. He began to recognize the complex emotions and challenges that each inmate faced, which helped him approach his role with greater sensitivity. By listening to their stories and understanding their struggles, Mark was able to offer more tailored and compassionate support. This newfound empathy also extended to his own self-reflection, as he gained a better understanding of the broader human experiences and emotions that contributed to his own journey of redemption.

3. Navigating the Complexities of Change

Through his mentorship role, Mark learned about the complexities of personal and social change. He realized that change was not a straightforward process and that each individual's path to rehabilitation was unique. Mark's experiences with his mentees highlighted the importance of flexibility and adaptability in providing effective support. He learned that change often required a combination of patience, understanding, and persistent effort.

4. Building Resilience

The challenges Mark faced in his mentorship role also contributed to his own resilience. The emotional and psychological demands of working with resistant inmates tested his commitment and fortitude. Mark's ability to persevere through these difficulties strengthened his resolve and reinforced his dedication to his role as a mentor. He learned to handle setbacks with a sense of resilience and to approach each challenge as an opportunity for growth.

5. Reflecting on His Own Journey

Mark's experiences with mentorship also prompted him to reflect on his own journey of change. He saw parallels between his own struggles and those of his mentees, which allowed him to approach his role with greater humility and understanding. Mark's reflections on his past mistakes and his current efforts at redemption provided him with valuable insights into the process of personal transformation.

The chapter closed with Mark contemplating the lessons he had learned through his mentorship role. Despite the difficulties and setbacks, he saw his experiences as a crucial part of his journey toward redemption. Mark recognized that the challenges he faced had contributed to his growth and had reinforced his commitment to making a positive impact on others. As he continued his role as a mentor, he remained dedicated to providing support and guidance, even in the face of adversity.

Chapter 14: Reflection on Crime

Introspection

As Mark Daniels approached the latter part of his sentence, he found himself increasingly drawn to a process of deep introspection. The journey of self-improvement and redemption he had embarked upon had led him to confront the painful reality of his past actions with greater clarity and honesty.

Mark spent hours in the quiet of his cell, reflecting on the series of events that had culminated in the robbery. He revisited the moment when he had made the fateful decision to participate in the crime, scrutinizing every detail with a mix of regret and sorrow. He delved into his motivations at that time—fear, desperation, and a misguided sense of pride. He had been a man struggling with financial pressures and personal insecurities, and these factors had clouded his judgment and led him down a dark path.

Mark also considered the broader societal influences that had contributed to his choices. He reflected on the systemic issues that had created an environment where crime seemed like a viable option for someone in his position. The economic disparity, lack of opportunity, and societal pressures were all part of the context that had influenced his decision-making. Mark's introspection led him to recognize the complex interplay between individual choices and systemic factors, providing him with a more nuanced understanding of his actions.

This period of reflection was both painful and illuminating. Mark grappled with the weight of his actions and the impact they had on his own life and the lives of others. The process of examining his past with such depth allowed him to confront the full extent of his mistakes and begin to reconcile with the consequences of his behavior.

Meeting with a Victim

A pivotal moment in Mark's journey of reflection came when he was given the opportunity to meet with a victim of his crime. The meeting was arranged through a restorative justice program, which aimed to facilitate dialogues between offenders and those affected by their crimes. For Mark, this meeting represented a chance to confront the reality of his actions and gain a deeper understanding of their impact.

The victim, an elderly man named Samuel, had been the store clerk during the robbery. Samuel had suffered both physical and emotional trauma as a result of the incident. The meeting took place in a controlled environment, with a mediator present to ensure that the conversation remained respectful and productive.

As Mark sat across from Samuel, he was struck by the gravity of the moment. Samuel's presence was a tangible reminder of the human cost of his actions. The elderly man's eyes carried the weight of his experience, and Mark could see the pain and apprehension that still lingered from the robbery.

During the meeting, Mark listened attentively as Samuel spoke about the impact of the crime on his life. Samuel recounted the fear and distress he had felt during the robbery and the ongoing emotional struggle he had faced since the incident. His words were filled with a mix of anger, hurt, and a desire for closure.

Mark's own emotions were intense as he listened. He felt a deep sense of remorse and guilt, and his heart ached as he heard about the lasting effects of his actions on Samuel's life. The conversation was an emotional rollercoaster, filled with moments of silence, tears, and heartfelt apologies.

In response, Mark expressed his sincere remorse and offered a heartfelt apology. He acknowledged the pain he had caused and conveyed his understanding of the suffering Samuel had endured. The dialogue was raw and honest, and it allowed both men to share their perspectives and emotions in a way that was both healing and confronting.

The meeting provided Mark with a profound sense of closure and a deeper understanding of the consequences of his crime. It was a moment of reckoning that allowed him to face the human impact of his actions and gain insight into the ways in which his behavior had affected others. This experience reinforced Mark's commitment to his journey of redemption and provided him with a renewed sense of purpose.

As the meeting concluded, Mark and Samuel parted with a sense of mutual respect and a shared understanding of the importance of reconciliation. The encounter was a significant step in Mark's path to making amends and moving forward with a greater sense of responsibility and empathy.

The chapter closed with Mark reflecting on the profound impact of the meeting and the lessons he had learned. The process of confronting the consequences of his actions had been both painful and transformative, and it had deepened his commitment to personal growth and redemption. Mark's journey of reflection and reconciliation continued as he moved forward with a renewed sense of purpose and a deeper understanding of the complexities of his past.

Chapter 15: Encounter with a Victim

Confrontation

Mark Daniels's journey toward redemption had been marked by numerous moments of self-reflection and personal growth, but nothing prepared him for the emotional weight of meeting someone directly affected by his crime. The opportunity arose through a restorative justice initiative aimed at fostering healing and understanding between offenders and victims or their families. Mark had volunteered to participate, driven by a deep desire to confront the full scope of his actions and seek a form of closure.

The meeting was set in a secure, neutral space, arranged with the assistance of a mediator who specialized in restorative justice. Mark arrived with a mixture of anxiety and resolve, knowing this encounter could be a turning point in his quest for redemption.

The individual he was about to meet was Laura Mitchell, a middle-aged woman whose husband, Robert, had been a store manager and a victim of the robbery. Robert had suffered significant physical injuries during the robbery, and the trauma had profoundly affected both him and Laura. Robert's health had never fully recovered, and Laura had been grappling with the emotional and financial fallout from the incident.

As Mark walked into the room, he saw Laura sitting quietly, her expression a mix of apprehension and determination. Laura had agreed to this meeting in the hope of finding some form of resolution and understanding. Mark was struck by the gravity of the situation, knowing that his actions had caused lasting pain for Laura and her family.

The initial moments were tense. Laura's eyes held a mixture of sadness and anger as she looked at Mark, her emotions raw and visible. Mark, too, felt a deep sense of vulnerability as he faced the person who had been directly affected by his crime. The mediator began by outlining the purpose of the meeting and ensuring both parties felt safe and heard.

Facing the Impact

As the conversation began, Laura shared her experience with Mark. She spoke of the night of the robbery, detailing the fear and confusion that had overwhelmed her husband and herself. Laura described the long road of recovery for Robert, the countless doctor visits, and the ongoing struggle with the emotional scars left by the attack. Her voice trembled as she recounted how the robbery had disrupted their lives, leaving them both physically and emotionally shattered.

Mark listened intently, his heart aching as he absorbed the weight of Laura's words. Each detail painted a vivid picture of the impact of his crime, forcing him to confront the pain and suffering he had caused. The raw honesty in Laura's account left Mark with a profound sense of regret and sorrow.

Laura's frustration and anger were palpable, and Mark understood the depth of her feelings. He tried to express his remorse, acknowledging that no words could ever fully make up for the harm he had inflicted. He shared his journey of self-reflection and the efforts he had made to change, hoping that his sincere remorse would be evident. Mark's voice wavered as he apologized, his eyes filled with tears of regret.

A Pivotal Moment

The meeting was a pivotal moment for Mark. It provided him with a direct and unfiltered view of the consequences of his actions, reinforcing the gravity of his past mistakes. The confrontation with Laura was both a painful and transformative experience, offering him a deeper understanding of the human cost of his crime.

Laura's response was mixed. She appreciated Mark's acknowledgment of the impact of his actions but also expressed the continued pain and difficulties she and her husband faced. The conversation did not offer a quick resolution or a complete sense of closure, but it allowed both Mark and Laura to share their perspectives and begin the process of healing.

As the meeting drew to a close, Mark and Laura exchanged a final, respectful nod. Mark felt a sense of closure, having faced the reality of his actions head-on and gained insight into the profound effects of his crime. Laura left the meeting with a sense of having been heard and a small step towards understanding and resolution.

Reflections and Growth

After the meeting, Mark reflected on the experience with a mixture of sorrow and gratitude. The encounter with Laura had been emotionally intense but had also reinforced his commitment to his path of redemption. He realized that the process of making amends was ongoing and that true reconciliation required continuous effort and understanding.

Mark's encounter with Laura became a significant chapter in his journey toward personal growth. It reinforced his sense of responsibility and the need to continue working towards positive change. The meeting provided him with a deeper sense of empathy and a renewed commitment to contributing positively to society.

As the chapter closed, Mark sat quietly in his cell, reflecting on the powerful experience of meeting Laura. He understood that while the path to redemption was challenging and complex, it was also filled with opportunities for growth and understanding. Mark's journey continued, marked by a profound sense of responsibility and a hopeful commitment to making amends for his past actions.

Chapter 16: Preparing for Release

Release Preparation

The final phase of Mark Daniels's incarceration was a time of intense focus and meticulous planning. Mark knew that transitioning from prison to the outside world would require not only practical preparation but also mental and emotional readiness. As he approached his release date, every aspect of his preparation was geared toward ensuring a successful reintegration into society.

1. Securing Housing

Securing stable housing was one of Mark's top priorities. Recognizing the critical role that a safe and supportive living environment would play in his reentry, Mark embarked on a thorough search for suitable housing options.

Research and Applications: Mark began by researching local housing options, including transitional housing programs and affordable rental units. He contacted various reentry organizations and non-profits specializing in assisting former inmates with finding housing. He meticulously filled out applications, often dealing with lengthy paperwork and multiple follow-ups. Each application was accompanied by a letter of support from his prison counselor, outlining his progress and commitment to reintegration.

Preparation for Independent Living: Mark also prepared himself for independent living by learning essential skills, such as budgeting, cooking, and managing household responsibilities. These skills were crucial for maintaining stability once he secured housing. He practiced these skills during his incarceration, often using commissary funds to buy ingredients and cooking meals in the prison kitchen.

Building Relationships: In addition to formal housing applications, Mark reached out to community organizations and local churches, seeking potential leads on affordable housing. He leveraged any connections he had made during his time in prison to explore potential housing options and gain support from local community members.

2. Planning for Employment

Finding meaningful employment was equally crucial for Mark's successful reintegration. Understanding that his criminal record could present significant barriers, Mark took proactive steps to prepare for the job market.

Vocational Training and Certifications: During his incarceration, Mark took advantage of vocational training programs offered by the prison. He earned certifications in fields such as carpentry and graphic design, areas that interested him and had potential for employment upon release. These programs not only provided him with practical skills but also boosted his confidence and sense of accomplishment.

Resume and Job Search: Mark dedicated time to crafting a professional resume that highlighted his new skills, personal growth, and commitment to positive change. He participated in job readiness workshops that focused on interview techniques, job search strategies, and addressing gaps in employment history. Mark also created a portfolio of his artwork, which he hoped could be a valuable asset in securing employment or freelance opportunities.

Networking and Support: Mark reached out to reentry programs that provided job placement services and career counseling. He attended job fairs and networking events organized for former inmates, where he connected with potential employers and mentors. His goal was to build relationships with individuals and organizations that could offer guidance and support as he navigated the job market.

3. Reconnecting with Support Networks

Rebuilding his life required not only practical preparation but also reconnecting with support networks that could offer assistance and encouragement.

Contacting Support Organizations: Mark reestablished contact with organizations and agencies that supported former inmates. He engaged with counselors, mentors, and support groups, discussing his plans for reentry and seeking advice on how to navigate the challenges he might face. These connections provided him with valuable resources and a sense of community.

Reconnecting with Personal Contacts: Mark also reached out to old friends and acquaintances who had supported him during his incarceration. He expressed his gratitude for their support and shared his plans for the future. Rebuilding these relationships was an important part of his reintegration, providing him with a support system and a network of people who believed in his potential.

Building New Connections: Mark made an effort to build new connections within the prison community that could continue to offer support after his release. He fostered relationships with mentors and peers who had successfully reintegrated into society, learning from their experiences and seeking their guidance.

Fears and Hopes

As the release date approached, Mark's emotions were a complex mix of fear, hope, and anticipation. The process of preparing for reentry involved grappling with numerous fears and uncertainties, while simultaneously holding onto a sense of hope for the future.

1. Societal Rejection

One of Mark's primary fears was the potential for societal rejection. He knew that his criminal record would be a significant hurdle, and he worried about how others would perceive him.

Stigma and Discrimination: Mark was aware of the stigma associated with having a criminal record, including potential difficulties in finding employment, securing housing, and rebuilding relationships. He anticipated facing prejudice and discrimination and prepared himself to address these challenges with resilience and determination.

Building a Positive Reputation: To counteract the negative perceptions, Mark focused on demonstrating his commitment to personal growth and positive change. He planned to share his story openly, emphasizing his journey of redemption and the steps he had taken to transform himself. Mark hoped that by highlighting his progress and contributions, he could begin to overcome the stigma and build a positive reputation.

2. Challenges of Rebuilding

Mark also recognized that rebuilding his life would involve numerous practical challenges.

Adjusting to Life Outside: The transition from the structured environment of prison to the freedoms and responsibilities of the outside world was daunting. Mark anticipated the need to adapt to new routines, manage daily responsibilities, and navigate a complex social landscape. He prepared for this adjustment by setting realistic goals and developing a plan to address potential obstacles.

Managing Finances: Mark understood that managing finances would be crucial for his stability. He planned to create a budget, set financial goals, and seek financial literacy resources to ensure he could manage his income effectively and avoid falling back into financial difficulties.

3. Hope for a Fresh Start

Amidst the fears and challenges, Mark held onto a strong sense of hope for a fresh start.

Vision for the Future: Mark envisioned a future where he could use his experiences and skills to make a positive impact on society. He dreamed of using his art to inspire others, contribute to community initiatives, and advocate for criminal justice reform. This vision provided him with motivation and a sense of purpose as he prepared for his release.

Support from Loved Ones: Mark's hope was also fueled by the potential for reconciliation with his family and the support of his community. He looked forward to rebuilding relationships and creating a new, positive chapter in his life. Mark's commitment to personal growth and his desire to contribute meaningfully to society were sources of optimism and strength.

Conclusion

As Mark's release date drew near, his preparations reflected a thoughtful and comprehensive approach to reentry. The practical steps he took, combined with his fears and hopes, shaped his outlook on the future. Mark's journey toward rebuilding his life was marked by careful planning, personal resilience, and a hopeful vision for a fresh start. His commitment to overcoming the challenges of reintegration and making a positive impact was a testament to his dedication to change and redemption.

Chapter 17: A New Vision

Future Goals

As Mark Daniels neared the end of his incarceration, he found himself contemplating a new vision for his life—one that reflected his growth, his aspirations, and his desire to make amends for his past actions. The experiences he had undergone during his time in prison, from discovering his artistic talent to participating in self-help groups and mentoring fellow inmates, shaped a clear and compelling vision for his future.

1. Using Art for Positive Impact

One of Mark's primary goals was to harness his passion for art to contribute positively to society. Art had been a lifeline for him during his imprisonment, providing an emotional outlet and a means of financial survival. Now, Mark envisioned using his artistic skills to inspire and uplift others, as well as to advocate for important causes.

Art Exhibitions and Sales: Mark planned to hold art exhibitions that would showcase his work and provide a platform for discussing themes of redemption, healing, and transformation. These exhibitions would not only offer him a chance to share his art with a broader audience but also create opportunities for dialogue about second chances and the potential for personal change.

Community Art Projects: Mark also envisioned engaging in community art projects that would benefit underserved neighborhoods and support local youth. By collaborating with schools, community centers, and non-profit organizations, he hoped to use art as a tool for education, empowerment, and social change.

Advocacy through Art: In addition to creating art, Mark aimed to use his work as a form of advocacy. He planned to support initiatives related to criminal justice reform, mental health awareness, and rehabilitation programs. His art could serve as a medium for raising awareness and fostering discussions about important social issues.

2. Personal and Professional Development

Mark's vision for his future extended beyond his artistic pursuits. He recognized the importance of personal and professional development in achieving a fulfilling and sustainable reintegration.

Continued Education: Mark intended to continue his education, either through formal academic programs or self-directed learning. He saw education as a way to enhance his skills, expand his knowledge, and increase his employability. Whether pursuing a degree, vocational training, or certifications, Mark was committed to ongoing learning and personal growth.

Career Goals: Alongside his artistic endeavors, Mark aimed to build a career that aligned with his values and interests. He considered exploring roles in community outreach, counseling, or advocacy—fields where he could use his experiences and skills to make a positive impact. Mark planned to network with professionals in these areas and seek mentorship to guide his career development.

Reentry Challenges

While Mark's vision for the future was clear and motivating, he was also acutely aware of the challenges that lay ahead. The process of reintegration into society posed several obstacles, and Mark prepared himself to face these challenges with resilience and determination.

1. Overcoming Stigma

One of the most significant challenges Mark anticipated was overcoming the stigma associated with his criminal record. The societal perception of former inmates often included bias and prejudice, which could impact his ability to secure employment, housing, and social acceptance.

Addressing Prejudice: Mark planned to confront stigma head-on by being open about his past and focusing on his personal growth and achievements. He understood that transparency and honesty were essential in building trust and demonstrating his commitment to positive change. Mark also sought to educate others about the importance of second chances and the potential for rehabilitation.

Building a Positive Reputation: To counteract negative perceptions, Mark aimed to actively engage in community service and advocacy work. By contributing to society and making a positive impact, he hoped to build a reputation based on his actions rather than his past mistakes. Mark believed that demonstrating his dedication to helping others would help reshape how he was perceived by the public.

2. Practical Challenges of Reentry

In addition to societal stigma, Mark faced practical challenges as he reintegrated into society. These included managing daily responsibilities, adjusting to life outside of prison, and navigating the complexities of reentry.

Adjusting to Life Outside: The transition from the structured environment of prison to the freedoms and responsibilities of the outside world required significant adjustment. Mark planned to address this by setting realistic goals, establishing a routine, and seeking support from reentry programs and mentors. He understood that adapting to life outside would be a gradual process and prepared himself to be patient and persistent.

Financial Stability: Ensuring financial stability was another critical aspect of Mark's reentry plan. He aimed to secure steady employment and manage his finances effectively to avoid falling into economic hardship. Mark's preparation included budgeting, financial planning, and seeking advice on managing his finances responsibly.

Conclusion

As Mark prepared for his release, his vision for the future was both ambitious and grounded in his experiences of personal growth. He saw his art as a powerful tool for positive impact and planned to use his skills and insights to contribute meaningfully to society. While he anticipated significant challenges in overcoming stigma and navigating the complexities of reintegration, Mark approached these challenges with a sense of hope and determination. His commitment to building a better future for himself and others reflected his dedication to making amends for his past and embracing the potential for redemption.

Chapter 18: Facing the World

Release Day

The day of Mark Daniels's release was a mixture of overwhelming emotions, each vying for dominance in his heart and mind. As he approached the moment of liberation, the culmination of his ten-year sentence, Mark experienced a complex array of feelings: anxiety, hope, and an undeniable sense of liberation.

1. The Anxiety of Transition

Mark's anxiety was palpable as the final hours of his incarceration ticked away. The anticipation of leaving the prison walls brought with it a cascade of worries and uncertainties.

Uncertainty About the Future: The transition from prison to the outside world was fraught with uncertainty. Mark had meticulously prepared for this day, but the reality of stepping into a new life brought doubts and fears. He wondered about the reception he would receive, the challenges he would face, and whether he could truly navigate the world outside.

Concerns About Rejection: The prospect of encountering societal rejection was a significant source of anxiety. Mark had spent years behind bars, and he was acutely aware that his criminal record might lead to prejudice and difficulty in securing employment and housing. The fear of being judged or stigmatized weighed heavily on him as he prepared to leave.

Adjusting to Freedom: The idea of freedom itself was both exhilarating and intimidating. Mark had been accustomed to the structured and controlled environment of prison life, and the sudden shift to personal autonomy was daunting. He worried about the practical aspects of living independently and the potential for feeling overwhelmed by the vast changes.

2. The Hope of a New Beginning

Despite the anxiety, Mark also felt a profound sense of hope and optimism. The prospect of starting anew, of rebuilding his life and contributing positively to society, was a powerful motivator.

Dreams of Redemption: Mark's dreams of redemption and making amends for his past fueled his hope. He envisioned using his art, his experiences, and his newfound skills to create a meaningful and positive impact. This vision provided him with a sense of purpose and direction as he faced the unknown.

Support and Encouragement: The support he received from reentry programs, mentors, and community organizations bolstered his hope. These sources of encouragement and guidance offered Mark reassurance and a sense of connection, helping him feel less alone as he ventured into a new phase of life.

Anticipation of Reconciliation: Mark also held onto the hope of reconnecting with his family. Although he knew that rebuilding relationships would take time, the possibility of mending his relationship with his estranged wife and daughter provided him with a sense of optimism and motivation.

Initial Reactions

As Mark walked out of the prison gates and into the outside world, the initial moments were a whirlwind of sensory and emotional experiences. The reality of freedom was both exhilarating and overwhelming.

1. Sensory Overload

The first steps outside the prison walls were marked by a sensory overload that Mark had not anticipated.

The Vastness of the World: The sheer expanse of the outside world contrasted sharply with the confines of prison. Mark marveled at the open sky, the bustling streets, and the vibrant colors of his surroundings. The freedom to move and explore was both exhilarating and daunting.

The Noise and Activity: The sounds and activity of the outside world were overwhelming. The constant hum of traffic, the chatter of people, and the cacophony of city life were a stark departure from the relative quiet of prison. Mark felt a mixture of excitement and disorientation as he adjusted to the new stimuli.

2. Mixed Reactions from Others

Mark's initial encounters with people outside the prison were a mix of positive and negative reactions.

Encounters with Strangers: Mark interacted with various individuals as he navigated his first day of freedom. Reactions from strangers ranged from curiosity and empathy to indifference and judgment. Some people offered kind words and encouragement, while others treated him with suspicion or disdain.

Support from Organizations: Mark's interactions with reentry organizations and support networks were more positive. Representatives from these organizations provided practical assistance, such as helping him with transportation and providing information about resources. Their support was a reassuring presence during his initial transition.

Challenges of Social Integration: The process of reintegrating into social settings was challenging. Mark found it difficult to gauge how to interact with others and navigate social norms that had evolved during his time in prison. He experienced moments of awkwardness and uncertainty as he reentered social spaces.

3. The Overwhelming Reality of Freedom

Mark's newfound freedom was both a blessing and a challenge. The responsibilities and opportunities that came with it were both exciting and daunting.

Managing Daily Responsibilities: Mark faced the immediate need to manage daily responsibilities, such as securing housing and finding employment. The practical aspects of daily life, which had been handled for him during his incarceration, now fell on his shoulders. This shift in responsibility added to the sense of pressure and urgency.

Facing Internal Doubts: Despite his preparations, Mark grappled with internal doubts about his ability to succeed. The fear of failure and the uncertainty of how to navigate this new phase of life were constant companions. He reminded himself of his goals and the steps he had taken to prepare, striving to maintain focus and resilience.

Conclusion

Mark's release day was a poignant moment of transition, marked by a complex blend of anxiety, hope, and the overwhelming reality of freedom. As he took his first steps into the outside world, the sensory overload and mixed reactions from others highlighted the challenges he would face. However, the support from reentry organizations and the hope for a new beginning provided him with a sense of direction and purpose. Mark's journey into freedom was a testament to his resilience and determination, setting the stage for the next chapter of his life as he faced the world with a renewed sense of possibility.

Chapter 19: Rebuilding Relationships

Family Reunion

After spending ten long years in prison, Mark Daniels's most profound hope was to reconnect with his estranged family. The anticipation of this reunion was fraught with a mix of excitement, fear, and uncertainty. The process of rebuilding these relationships would be complex, marked by emotional highs and lows, and would require patience, understanding, and a willingness to face painful truths.

1. Reaching Out

Mark's first step was to reach out to his ex-wife, Sarah, and their daughter, Emily. He carefully drafted letters and made phone calls, trying to convey his heartfelt apologies, explain his journey, and express his sincere desire to rebuild their relationship.

Letters and Phone Calls: Mark wrote several letters to Sarah, detailing his experiences, personal growth, and the steps he had taken to change his life. He sent photographs of his art and described how it had helped him find meaning and purpose. He hoped these letters would bridge the gap created by years of separation and help Sarah and Emily understand his transformation.

Phone Call Anxiety: The phone calls with Sarah were emotionally charged. They began with awkward pauses and strained conversation, as they both grappled with the unfamiliarity of speaking after so long. Mark's voice trembled with emotion as he tried to articulate his remorse and hope for reconciliation.

2. The Reunion

The reunion with his daughter, Emily, was particularly poignant. Mark had not seen her since she was a young child, and she was now a teenager.

Emotional Encounter: The first meeting was a mix of tears, awkward silence, and tentative gestures. Emily was guarded, unsure of how to relate to the father she barely knew. Mark's attempts to connect were met with a mixture of curiosity and skepticism. He was sensitive to her feelings and understood that rebuilding their bond would take time.

Gradual Healing: Over time, their interactions began to soften. Mark made efforts to engage in activities Emily enjoyed, listen to her concerns, and share moments of vulnerability. He respected her boundaries and allowed her to express her feelings without judgment. Slowly, Emily began to open up, and they started to rediscover their connection.

3. Sarah's Struggle

Sarah's reactions to Mark's return were complex. She experienced a whirlwind of emotions—anger, sadness, confusion, and a reluctant glimmer of hope.

Processing Emotions: Sarah struggled with the pain and betrayal she felt from Mark's absence. The years of hardship and the burden of raising Emily alone had left her scarred. While she appreciated Mark's efforts to make amends, she found it difficult to reconcile the man she knew with the person he had become.

Building Trust: Trust was a significant issue. Sarah was cautious and skeptical of Mark's intentions. It took time for her to see the sincerity of his efforts and the changes he had undergone. Gradually, through consistent actions and open communication, Mark began to rebuild her trust.

Community Involvement

As Mark settled into his new life, he turned his focus to community involvement, recognizing the importance of contributing positively to society and finding purpose beyond his personal relationships.

1. Engaging with Support Organizations

Mark sought out organizations that supported former inmates and at-risk youth, eager to use his experiences and skills to make a difference.

Volunteering: He volunteered at local non-profits that provided support and resources for people reintegrating into society. His role involved offering mentorship, sharing his story, and helping others navigate the challenges of reentry. Mark found fulfillment in helping others avoid the pitfalls he had encountered.

Art Workshops: Mark organized and participated in art workshops for at-risk youth, using his artistic talents to engage and inspire young people. He believed that art could be a powerful tool for self-expression and healing, and he aimed to provide a positive outlet for those who might be struggling.

2. Advocacy and Outreach

Mark also became involved in advocacy efforts, focusing on criminal justice reform and rehabilitation.

Public Speaking: He began speaking at community events, sharing his journey of redemption and the lessons he had learned. His talks emphasized the importance of second chances, the value of rehabilitation, and the need for supportive systems for former inmates.

Supporting Reform Initiatives: Mark collaborated with organizations advocating for criminal justice reform. He participated in panels, contributed to discussions on policy changes, and worked to raise awareness about the challenges faced by formerly incarcerated individuals.

3. Building a New Identity

In addition to his community involvement, Mark worked on building a new identity for himself—one that reflected his growth, values, and aspirations.

New Social Circles: Mark made an effort to connect with new people and build positive relationships outside of his past. He joined local clubs, attended community events, and sought to form connections based on shared interests and values.

Personal Fulfillment: Mark continued to pursue personal fulfillment through his art, education, and community work. He set goals for his future, focused on maintaining a positive lifestyle, and strived to contribute meaningfully to his community.

Conclusion

The process of rebuilding relationships and engaging with the community was both challenging and rewarding for Mark. The reunion with his family was marked by emotional complexity and gradual healing, requiring patience and understanding from all parties involved. His commitment to community involvement and advocacy provided him with a sense of purpose and fulfillment, as he worked to make a positive impact and forge a new path. Mark's journey was a testament to the power of redemption, the importance of second chances, and the potential for personal transformation.

Chapter 20: The First Steps

Career and Art

With the initial challenges of reintegration behind him, Mark Daniels began to build his life anew, focusing on two central areas: his career and his art. These became the cornerstones of his new identity, driving his efforts to establish a meaningful and fulfilling life.

1. Establishing a Career in Art

Mark's art had been a vital part of his rehabilitation journey, and now it became a significant part of his professional life. He found creative ways to turn his passion into a sustainable livelihood.

Art Exhibitions: Mark organized several art exhibitions to showcase his work. These exhibitions were held in local galleries, community centers, and even online platforms. Each exhibit was meticulously curated to reflect the themes of redemption, loss, and hope that had characterized his journey. The exhibitions drew attention from local media and the art community, helping to establish Mark's reputation as a serious artist.

Commissioned Work: As Mark's reputation grew, he began receiving commissions for his art. He worked on private projects for individuals and collaborated with organizations to create pieces for public spaces. The commissions provided him with a steady income and allowed him to continue his artistic expression while contributing to various causes.

Art Therapy Workshops: Mark also started leading art therapy workshops for individuals who had experienced trauma or were struggling with personal challenges. These workshops were designed to provide a therapeutic outlet through creative expression, drawing on Mark's own experiences with art as a form of healing.

2. Community Projects

Mark's commitment to community service was a natural extension of his desire to give back and make a positive impact.

Collaborative Art Projects: He initiated collaborative art projects with local schools and community groups. These projects involved creating large-scale murals, organizing art fairs, and engaging community members in artistic endeavors. The goal was to foster a sense of community and provide creative opportunities for people of all ages.

Mentorship Programs: Mark used his experience and skills to mentor young artists and individuals facing similar challenges. He offered guidance, encouragement, and practical advice, helping them navigate their own journeys and find their own paths to success.

Public Speaking

Alongside his artistic endeavors, Mark embraced public speaking as a way to share his story and advocate for change. His speeches became a powerful tool for promoting themes of redemption, change, and the importance of second chances.

1. Speaking Engagements

Local and Regional Events: Mark was invited to speak at various local and regional events, including schools, community organizations, and conferences focused on criminal justice reform and rehabilitation. His talks were candid and heartfelt, drawing from his personal experiences and the lessons he had learned.

Educational Institutions: Mark also spoke at educational institutions, sharing his story with students and faculty. These engagements aimed to provide insights into the challenges of incarceration, the potential for personal transformation, and the importance of supportive systems for those reintegrating into society.

2. Themes and Messages

Redemption and Personal Growth: Mark's speeches emphasized the power of redemption and personal growth. He spoke about the steps he took to change his life, the challenges he faced, and the importance of self-reflection and perseverance.

The Importance of Second Chances: A central theme in Mark's public speaking was the value of second chances. He advocated for more compassionate approaches to criminal justice and emphasized the need for support systems that enable formerly incarcerated individuals to rebuild their lives.

Inspiration and Hope: Mark's story served as an inspiration for many. He highlighted the potential for positive change and the capacity for individuals to overcome their pasts and contribute meaningfully to society. His message was one of hope and resilience, encouraging others to pursue their own paths to redemption.

3. Media and Advocacy

Media Appearances: Mark's growing prominence led to appearances in local media and interviews where he shared his journey and discussed his advocacy work. These opportunities helped amplify his message and reach a broader audience.

Advocacy Campaigns: Mark became involved in advocacy campaigns aimed at promoting criminal justice reform and supporting rehabilitative programs. He used his platform to raise awareness about the challenges faced by former inmates and the need for systemic change.

Conclusion

Mark's first steps into his new life were marked by a combination of creative achievement and public advocacy. His career in art not only provided him with a means of livelihood but also allowed him to contribute to his community and support others on their own journeys. His public speaking efforts helped spread his message of redemption, change, and the importance of second chances. As Mark continued to navigate his new path, he remained focused on using his experiences to inspire and make a positive impact, embodying the transformative power of personal growth and redemption.

Epilogue: The Journey Continues

As Mark Daniels stood in front of a large canvas in his studio, he felt a profound sense of reflection. The artwork he was creating was a tribute to his journey—a visual representation of the trials, growth, and redemption that had defined his years of incarceration and reintegration into society. Each brushstroke was imbued with meaning, each color representing a chapter of his life.

1. Reflection on the Journey

Mark's journey had been anything but straightforward. The path from incarceration to reintegration had been fraught with obstacles, personal demons, and the constant struggle to redefine himself. Yet, as he looked back, he saw more than just the pain and challenges; he saw resilience and growth.

Acknowledging the Challenges: Mark recognized the immense difficulties he had faced—loss of identity, isolation, and the struggle to rebuild relationships. He remembered the nights spent battling his inner demons, the heartache of estrangement from his family, and the relentless effort to overcome the stigma of his past. Each challenge had shaped him and contributed to his evolution.

Celebrating Growth: Despite the hardships, Mark took pride in the person he had become. His commitment to art, his involvement in the community, and his dedication to personal growth were testament to his progress. The transformative power of his journey was evident in his achievements and the impact he had made on others.

2. Ongoing Struggles

Even as Mark embraced his newfound purpose and success, he understood that his journey was far from over. Redemption and personal transformation were ongoing processes, not destinations.

Facing the Past: Mark continued to grapple with the scars of his past. The memories of his crime and the pain he had caused lingered, serving as a constant reminder of the importance of continued growth and self-improvement. He knew that confronting his past and learning from it was an ongoing necessity.

Navigating the Future: As he moved forward, Mark faced the realities of reintegration. The challenge of overcoming societal stigma and finding his place in the world was a daily struggle. He remained aware of the need to remain vigilant and proactive in maintaining the positive changes he had made.

3. Hope for the Future

Despite the challenges, Mark held onto a sense of hope and optimism. His journey had taught him that redemption was not a final destination but a continuous process of growth and contribution.

Vision for the Future: Mark envisioned a future where he could further his impact through his art and advocacy. He hoped to expand his community projects, mentor more individuals, and continue to inspire others with his story. His goals included creating more platforms for dialogue and support for those struggling with similar issues.

Continued Impact: Mark was committed to using his experiences to make a positive difference. He planned to keep sharing his story, advocating for change, and working on projects that could foster understanding and support for former inmates. His journey was an evolving narrative, one that he intended to keep shaping through his actions and contributions.

4. The Story Unfolds

As the final touches were added to his painting, Mark reflected on the idea that his story was still unfolding. Redemption was not a finite achievement but an ongoing journey marked by moments of reflection, growth, and continued effort.

A Living Journey: Mark understood that his life was a living journey, with each day offering new opportunities for learning and growth. The story of his transformation was dynamic and ever-evolving, and he embraced the idea that he would continue to write it through his choices and actions.

Message of Hope: In closing, Mark's message was one of hope and perseverance. His story illustrated that change was possible, that redemption was achievable, and that the path to a better future was paved with continuous effort and a willingness to confront and learn from one's past.

Mark stepped back from the canvas, taking a moment to appreciate the journey that had brought him to this point. The painting was more than just an artwork; it was a reflection of his life's narrative—a story of struggle, growth, and the relentless pursuit of redemption. As he looked at the completed piece, he felt a profound sense of peace and purpose, ready to face the future with hope and determination.

The End

www.ingramcontent.com/pod-product-compliance
Lightning Source LLC
Chambersburg PA
CBHW071958210526
45479CB00003B/987